Intellectual Engagement:

Reflections on the First Twenty Five Years of the Association of Muslim Social Scientists

Compiled and Edited by

Iqbal J. Unus

DEDICATION

To the pioneers of the Association of Muslim Social Scientists, and those who followed in their footsteps.

ACKNOWLEDGMENT

Articles in this collection are personal reflections by some of those who pioneered and sustained the growth of the Association of Muslim Social Scientists (AMSS) during its first twenty-five years. There are many others who deserve recognition and gratitude for their initiative and dedication, as authors in this collection point out.

Authors have not been asked to update or revise their reflections in any way since they were originally written over two decades ago in 1996. All articles are reproduced here without any changes, except for a few inadvertent typing or grammatical errors or inconsistencies.

All opinions expressed in this collection are those of the authors and do not necessarily reflect the opinions or views of the Association of Muslim Social Scientists or of the compiler/editor.

CONTENTS

Association of Muslim Social Scientists

INTRODUCTION

Iqbal J. Unus

The founding of the Muslim Students Association of the United States and Canada (MSA) in 1963 was a momentous event during the growing Muslim presence in North America. Following Muslim predecessors who had made their home in this land over the centuries, a new corps of student arrivals – swelling in numbers after the 1965 immigration reforms – introduced new dimensions in outlook, purpose and lifestyle of Muslims in America. Well educated in their homelands and aiming to further their education in the crucible of quality higher education, they set a tone distinctly different from the earlier arrivals. Spread on college campuses throughout the land, they created a network of thoughts and ideas about the intersection of their faith and culture and their newly acquired knowledge and understanding of modern day social sciences that was essentially anchored in a different worldview.

These students graduated from colleges and graduate schools and while some returned to their homelands, many stayed behind and started their careers in the American academia. They soon realized that their

1

network of ideas needed to be given life through a professional scholarly society of professors and students of academic disciplines in social sciences. They also realized that the expanding Muslim presence needed more than religious education and community outreach. It needed a deeper understanding of the society they were becoming a part of, and to whose intellectual underpinning they had a responsibility to contribute from their own faith perspective. It needed an Islam-based forum for intellectual engagement, a channel for integrating Islamic principles and perspectives within academic disciplines. That realization led to laying the foundation of the Association of Muslim Social Scientists (AMSS) in 1971, which was officially registered in the Commonwealth of Pennsylvania in 1972 with the distinguished professor Ismail Ragi Al-Faruqi as is its first president, who remained in office for three terms.

In its early documents, AMSS stated its purpose to be "to stimulate scholarly thinking and research and carry out studies designed to develop an Islamic scientific methodology and seek Islamic solutions to contemporary problems …"

Since its beginnings AMSS has regularly held annual conferences, hosted each year by different academic institutions in the United States, including several ivy league universities.

The first AMSS annual conference was held at the University of Indianapolis (then known as Indiana Central College) in 1972. The twenty-fifth annual conference of AMSS was held in 1996 at the School of Islamic and Social Sciences in Leesburg, VA. As conference chairman, I requested some of its past presidents to share their reflections on the first twenty five years of this unique organization. They were generous in their responses, which were shared with conference participants as a part of the conference program.

A part of the historical record of AMSS, these first-hand accounts of the Association in its first twenty five years can be a useful resource for researchers interested in the growth of the American Muslim community. This collection now makes them available to academics and non-academics to contemplate on the challenges and prospects that the early leaders of AMSS saw as they strived to blend the disciplines of social sciences with the overarching worldview of their faith.

Dr. Mushtaqur Rahman, president in 1996, wrote The President's Message. Dr. AbdulHamid AbuSulayman, Dr. Dilnawaz Siddiqui, Dr. Sulayman

Nyang and Dr. Anis Ahmad – all former presidents – wrote other articles. Sad to say, Dr. Rahman and Dr. Siddiqui have since passed away. The affiliation of each author at the time of the silver jubilee of AMSS is listed with his article of reflection. As of this writing, Dr. AbdulHamid AbuSulayman is president of IIIT, Dr. Anis Ahmad is president of Riphah University, and Dr. Sulayman Nyang is professor at Howard University.

In the early 1980s, AMSS developed intellectual collaboration with the International Institute of Islamic Thought (IIIT). Until 2013, AMSS and IIIT jointly published the quarterly *American Journal of Islamic Social Sciences* (AJISS), which covers research on various aspects of Islam and the Muslim world, and on the intersection of rational academic thinking with the Islamic belief system. [AJISS continues to be published by IIIT after 2013.]

Following its silver jubilee in 1996, AMSS continued to march forward in the fulfillment of its mission through its annual conferences and its journal until 2013 when North American Association of Islam and Muslim Studies (NAAIMS) took over some of its functions.

REFLECTIONS

Readers are researchers are advised that all opinions expressed in this collection are those of the authors and do not necessarily reflect the opinions or views of the Association of Muslim Social Scientists or of the compiler/editor.

1 THE PRESIDENT'S MESSAGE

Dr. Mushtaqur Rahman[1]

It is my pleasure to welcome you to Herndon on behalf of the Association of Muslim Social Scientists (AMSS), and on my own behalf. I know that this conference will be a milestone in providing you a forum to interact constructively and to compare our ideas and efforts.

I know the program committee has done everything possible to make the conference stimulating and academically rewarding. In spite of all the handicaps the secretary of the Program Committee of AMSS has done a splendid job.

Alhamdullilah, this year AMSS is twenty-five years old. During these long years. AMSS faced many obstacles and challenges. We in AMSS took every challenge as an opportunity to grow further in a positive manner, like our founder-brothers did for us. A worldwide network of AMSS, a prestigious quarterly journal, the school of Islamic and social sciences (SISS), international conferences overseas,

---

[1] *Dr. Mushtaqur Rahman is professor of cultural Geography at Iowa State University, Ames, Iowa*

and efforts to Islamize knowledge are some examples.

These and other related activities were directed to present a peaceful and amicable Muslim world view to those who Muslims and Islam with a different perspective.

The Muslims still have two images in the West - both bleak, and both unrealistic. The first is the notion that Muslims are militant, aggressive, and brutal. The second relates to Islamic revivalism in Egypt, Turkey, Indonesia, Afghanistan or other parts of the Muslim World, which is considered a threat to civilization, the ruination of national states, and every type of civic mutuality. Following this assumption, the western print and telecommunication outlets presents Muslims as aggressive and brutal so powerfully that nationality and facts go under.

Muslims often resent this erroneous portrayal of themselves and their civilization, and rightly so. A number of papers received for annual conferences cataloged Muslim stereotypes or lamented adverse comments of the media giving examples from our glorious past. To counter these examples our critics said that the Muslims are living in history, in monuments, and in memories. They have nothing compatible to the contemporary world. If we join AMSS and unite in examining and identifying what each Muslim social scientist does best and capitalize on it, we can turn our history into a living history. With this in mind, and to know our human resources around the world, AMSS is embarking on compilation of a resource directory of the Muslim world. If we all unite, we can take charge of this change to living history.

This is the time when I should apologize for our shortcomings and present my thanks to all of you and other supporters of AMSS, especially the International Institute of Islamic Thought, the Islamic Society of North America, and other Muslim organizations.

2 ASSOCIATION OF MUSLIM SOCIAL SCIENTISTS: 1971-1996

AbdulHamid AbuSulayman[2]

I am thankful to the Association of Muslim Social Scientists (AMSS) for inviting me, as an old and founding member of AMSS to contribute an article to this program published in commemoration of AMSS' 25th anniversary in order to shed some light on its background.

It is very pleasing to see that after twenty-five years, AMSS is still contributing to the noble cause of Islamization of knowledge. The most encouraging aspect is to see that the Association is *Alhamdullilah* still expanding, taking deeper roots, and reaching out to the Muslim intellectuals.

It may be useful for younger members and contributors to understand some basic aspects of it history, that is, the reasons for its establishment, goals set for it, and the scope it may have. This hopefully will strengthen the commitment of its members and provide continuity and effectiveness to

---

[2] *Dr. AbdulHamid AbuSulayman is Rector of the International Islamic University Malaysia*

harness its objectives, *in sha'Allah*.

It may be crucial for its members and supporters to understand that AMSS, as an organization, is a movement and part of the larger response of the ummah's cultural renaissance to the alien cultural invasion and its threats to its Islamic identity.

After about three hundred years since the Ottoman caliphate, Egypt, and then followed by many other Muslim States, the *ummah* tried to revive its strength and capabilities.

These reforms started with the establishment of schools and institutions of science and technology (engineering), modernization, of military, adoption of the western liberal thought, introduction of nationalism, secularism, multi-party system, one-party system, state control, socialism, and totalitarianism. The results, thus far are clearly a shocking failure. This undoubtedly indicates, and obviously shows, that these reforms were cosmetic and superficial, and that there are deeper causes for the decline of the *ummah*. Motivation is the only way through which Muslims can achieve real and deep changes in the psychological and mental attitude of the *ummah* which could enable it to regain its strength, change its old ways, and shed the crippling fears and apprehensions deeply embedded in the traditional Muslim psyche.

With this bleak picture and background of failures, I was, like many other Muslims, wondering about this dilemma, hoping to find new ways and solutions for the *ummah's* ills and weakness.

Having exposure to somewhat wide Islamic and contemporary knowledge, the rich library of my family, and the cultural atmosphere of my hometown, Makkah, with modern education in commerce, political science and international relations, provided me with an ample opportunity to grasp the appalling conditions of the contemporary Muslim world. It is not difficult to notice that the common factors between the poor and the weak Muslim peoples, whether in the north or the south or whether in the majority or the minority, are only cultural.

Knowing that the Muslim world does not lack resources or noble goals and values of Islam has clearly led me to identify that only the psychological, intellectual, and mental dimensions of the Muslim personality and culture are the actual causes behind its weakness and ills.

What specifically led me to propose the establishment of AMSS in the year 1391H/1971AD to my fellow leading members of the Muslim Students' Association of US and Canada was my exposure to certain direct experiences. The first one was a book which I published in 1380H/1960 entitled; *"The Islamic Theory of Economics: its Philosophy and Contemporary Means."* In this book I approached the subject in a clear and non-traditional way which produced a totally different, encouraging, and unconventional result. The conclusions in this book made me see Islam more relevant to the contemporary world. These conclusions suggested basic and ambitious change in the Muslim world's economic philosophy and its approach to the system. I did realize then that the reason I was able to produce such work was the professional aspect in my systematic and methodological formal academic education which was coupled with wide and free variety of readings through the family library on modern and old Islamic literature. The methodology I used in this book was more of the methodology of contemporary social sciences by being comprehensive, empirical, analytical and systematic. Naturally, this led me to consider the time-space factors of the early Muslim model and to realize and understand the policy factor in the prophet (SAW)'s traditions and directions to his people during that Islamic model.

The second encounter in 1960 which led me to call for the reform of Muslim thought, and to emphasize on its methodological aspects, was my experience as a student of humanities with the Muslim and the nationalist students' movement. It was a very turbulent time of struggle between the nationalist and leftist groups and the Islamic groups. The qualities and training of each other gave me a clear understanding of the immediate reasons behind their polarization and conflict between and for the absence of young, active, social scientists in various fields of the Islamic organizations, who are mostly physical scientists and the members and supporters of the secular, nationalist, liberal, and leftist movements and organizations who were mostly social and human scientists.

It happened that during one of my years of studies at the university of Pennsylvania, I was both the president of MSA, and the president of the Arab students' organizations chapter of the university of Pennsylvania and Philadelphia. Observing members of both organizations confirmed the dichotomy that I had already realized. The majority of the members from the Islamic organization were from physical and natural sciences while the members from social studies and humanities were in the minority. However, the situation in the secular-oriented organizations was the opposite.

My cultural and academic background, which I have already mentioned, and the actual experience with the Arab and Muslim students made it clear that we should seek deeper intellectual solutions, and for that, I propose the idea of establishing an intellectual forum: the Association of Muslim Social Scientist (AMSS). The association was to get the Muslim intellectuals together to work for reform of the proper psyche attitude, Islamic thought, methodology, and to develop the Islamic contemporary knowledge to generate workable and viable attitudes, thoughts, ideas, and solutions to serve contemporary societies and Muslim life. The methodological reform should, no doubt, be able to create healthy common culture and communicable intellectual language for the benefit of the Muslim mind. This should make the Islamic *Tawhidic* and *khilafah* concepts provide clear, dynamic, practical, and workable guidance for Muslim life. This, no doubt, will also help solve many of the problems of the confused materialistic contemporary human civilization.

The cause of dichotomy and of lack of common language is that the Muslim students, who are mostly physical scientist, stop at the general and broad theoretical aspects of belief (*Aqidah*) of Islam and follow half-heartedly the rules of Islamic traditions and jurisprudence. Their contemporary writings used to be mostly non-professional. They are usually busy with their scientific and professional work and see no need to go deeper to discover intellectually.

Because of the nature of their field of study, the students of social sciences and humanities have different level of intellectual demands and expectations. They are the students who are in the midst of the intellectual and contemporary way of life and civilization. They cannot stop at the general and theoretical aspect and ideas. Their training requires more concrete and workable thoughts and ideas.

Unfortunately, the Islamic literature in many ways was and still to a certain extent is basically produced with little professional knowledge. Most of these traditional or general authors do not really comprehend this complexity of issues at hand. They mostly produce either archaic or superficial ideas and pictures, which in practical terms do not help the cause of Islam and the Muslim mind in the contemporary world. This superficial treatment does not cure the deep causes for Muslim mind in the contemporary world. This superficial treatment does not cure the deep causes of Muslim ills and does not help to reform the Muslim mind, thoughts, and psychology. This, to a great extent explains the reason why most Muslim social scientists do not show appreciation and enthusiasm for Islamic thought and movement.

As a student of social sciences, I do believe that real solutions to this dilemma are psychological and intellectual, if we are seriously going to embark upon real and workable social and civilizational reform. Muslim thought should gain its dynamism. Muslim psychology should gain its courage and healthy and positive attitude towards life and beyond, and should recapture its comprehension of space and time. *Aqidah* should be taken as a source of strength and a base for a dynamic and progressive Muslim social system.

The Association of Muslim Social Scientist held its inaugural conference in 1972 to serve methodological reform of the contemporary Islamic thought. The late Shaheed Dr. Ismail al-Faruqi, professor of comparative religion in Temple University in Philadelphia, Pennsylvania, was elected first president of the Association. His sincerity, intellectual capabilities, respected academic position, and excellent command of the English Language served the Association and its noble goals extremely well during its early and tender age.

I was convinced that a full-time institution is needed to complement and serve the Islamic goals of AMSS. In 1401/1981, the registration of the International Institute of Islamic Thought (IIIT) was in fact establishing a full-time AMSS and IIIT. The actual opening of its offices in 1983 marked a new era of serving Islamic thought both through AMSS and IIIT and through the conferences, publications, and a joint journal called *The American Journal of Islamic Social Sciences* (AJISS). It was a great honor for me to serve this noble cause as the first president of IIIT (1981-1984) and as the director general of IIT and president of AMSS (1984-1988).

In 1985, I concentrated on producing a new Arabic Edition of the IIIT work plan entitled *"Islamization of knowledge."* The first edition was written by Prof. Ismail al-Faruqi. I also supervised the translation of Arabic edition to English. During this period, I also put together my book *"Crisis in the Muslim Mind"* out of many papers I had delivered in different Islamic conferences.

In December 1988, I left for Malaysia to reorganize and develop the international Islamic University Malaysia (IIUM). Through this period until now,

AMSS has continued to grow and gain prominence in serving the intellectual Islamic cause of Islamization of knowledge. This was possible because of the dedication and determination of the leaders and members of this noble association.

The road ahead is still long and difficult for Islamic social scientists, IIIT, AMSS, and IIUM in order to prove the worthiness, and to gain the dynamism and relevance, of contemporary Islamic thought to the actual challenges of Muslim needs, life, and societies.

Islamic social scientists, with their professionalism and Islamic knowledge, and the right methodology, would no doubt bring back to real life the *aqidah* and concepts of *tawheed, khilafah, shura', takaful,* and justice to guide Muslim thought and to provide a solid base for workable systems, institutions, and solutions for new Muslim dynamic societies. A methodological and well-reformed Islamic thought should be able to effectively address man as an integrated totality of material, moral and spiritual being, free from dichotomies and conflicts of contemporary thought and civilization.

I hope that this brief account of the early days of AMSS will bring understanding and stronger commitment to its noble mission.

I pray to Allah (SWT) to provide us all with the strength and success in the service of life, *ummah* and Islam.

3 REFLECTIONS ON AMSS

Dilnawaz Siddiqui[3]

I would like to join the entire membership of the Association of Muslim Social Scientists (AMSS) and other well wishers of it in thanking Allah (SWT) for all its accomplishments and enabling all of us to have weathered the odds in surviving so far.

Our Association has come a long way in improving the quality of its journal - The American Journal of Islamic Social Sciences (AJISS) - and in bringing AJISS' frequency from three to four issues per year. It has also succeeded in attracting new and younger social scientists to contribute to it with considerable regularity. As a result, it is now regarded as an authentic resource on Islamic perspectives of various social science disciplines. It is also gratifying to see many Muslims social scientists engaged in institution building and organizational development in different parts of the *ummah*.

However, besides such congratulatory statements, we need to critically evaluate our performance in

---

[3] **Dr. Dilnawaz Siddiqui is Professor of Communication at Clarion University of Pennsylvania, Clarion, Pennsylvania.*

terms of the extent to which we have accomplished
its original mission of producing a cadre of scholars
well-versed in the contending paradigms and their
ontological, epistemological, meta-theoretical, as well
as methodological components. We need to ask
ourselves whether or not we have succeeded in
producing scholarly instructional and reference
materials from a valid and comprehensive (Islamic)
perspective in our respective discipline areas. One
can argue that the Islamization of knowledge
mission is ongoing. But there is no denying the fact
that the outcome so far may not be commensurate
with the quarter of a century's worth of time and
energy. Our infancy seems to have persisted or
prolonged for various reasons.

A professional association, in order for it to succeed,
calls for self-reliance in terms of human, financial,
and organizational resources. To the extent of North
America and that of the immigrant Muslim
community, the number of social scientist as
compared to pure and applied physical and
biological professionals has been inordinately
limited. Moreover, we have been struggling to
survive in a tight job market and we have not yet
made a concerted effort to sensitize the broader
Muslim community to the need of the Association.
The traditional sources of financial and

organizational support have undergone and are undergoing a severe constraint. Among the hardcore persistent volunteers, one can notice the measure of alienation and frustration with their limitations to enthuse younger social scientists to get involved. There is a need to look into reasons for the withdrawal syndrome of some old quads and the hesitancy of the younger ones.

There is a dire need to launch a serious membership campaign, to reach out to communities to explain AMSS mission, goals and objectives, and to explore areas of cooperation and collaboration. These things are to be communicated to the non-social scientists in non-technical terms by stressing the importance of the potential services and guidance the social scientists can provide to them. Dr. Ilyas Bayunus' demographic studies in Illinois, management training efforts by Dr. Rafik Beekun and others, as well as instructional and curricular inputs of many in various communities, are worthy ventures worth emulating.

These activities do not fall in the purview of theoretical development of AMSS. However, from the Islamic perspective, the ultimate goal of knowledge is to help resolve practical human problems: spiritual, educational, social, political, and economic. Researchers are supposed to provide the activists with data to facilitate proper and timely decision making in tackling the multifarious challenges facing the *ummah*. The more urgent the crisis, the more practical social scientists need to be. Under such circumstances, mere theoretical discussions are tantamount to ivory tower escapism. Generation and documentation of practical measures to solve the problems ought to be the primary concern of all of us. Let theories be derived from the experiences after the crisis have dissipated. For instance, most management literature based on case studies has evolved as a result of documenting the positive and negative experiences of managers. Even in the ideal situations, formulation of practical solutions of present and potential problems in various walks of life and derivation of scientific principles and models go on concurrently.

On the organizational support level, the powers that be need to be realistic in their expectations, respectful of volunteer efforts of those who contribute their valuable time, energy and other resources in a sincere pursuit of the pleasure of Allah (SWT), and thankful for their services howsoever small. The prophetic saying in this regard is: Those who are thankless to people are thankless to Allah.

May Allah guide us along the right path and bless

our efforts with success in further developing the Association of Muslim Social Scientists and in serving His cause with honesty, sincerity, dedication, and to our utmost capabilities!

4 REFLECTIONS ON THE SILVER JUBILEE OF AMSS

Sulayman Nyang[4]

1 996 is an important year for the leadership and the membership of the Association of Muslim Social Scientists in the United States of America and Canada (AMSS). It was almost twenty-five years ago, when a number of Muslim intellectuals mainly centered in the social science gathered to examine political, social, and economic issues confronting the Muslim world. Drawing upon their respective disciplines, and hoping to advance the frontiers of knowledge within the Muslim world and beyond, this small group of Muslims intellectuals in the U.S and Canada launched an organization that was North American in origin but global in outreach and objectives. That is to say, those who founded AMSS had a global perspective and their record certainly testifies to this fact. Driven by the need to give legitimacy to the growing number of Muslims living and working within the American society, and seriously concerned about their Islamic identity in a

---

[4] *Dr. Sulayman Nyang is professor of African studies at Howard University, Washington,D.C.*

world that was going through rapid and unprecedented changes, these founding fathers of AMSS saw to it that an organization came into being and that Muslims with any familiarity with the social sciences were recruited to attend its annual meetings. It was indeed this exercise in recruitment of new members and new contributors to the various panels organized at annual meetings of the organization that opened the door to me and many others in the early eighties. To be more precise, it was my fortunate encounter with brother Mumtaz Ahmed that led to my initiation into AMSS. Brother Mumtaz, who is now Dr. Ahmed at Hampton University's Political Science Department, was then a visiting fellow at the Brookings Institution in Washington, D.C.

Since that fateful encounter with Dr. Ahmed many good things have happened to me in my love affair with AMSS. After almost a year of association with the organization I came to know a wide range of Muslim scholars and intellectuals interested in the social sciences. Seven major developments have taken place in my life since my initial encounter with AMSS and its membership. The first matter of significance was my greater involvement with the activities of the MSA chapters around the country. By becoming active in AMSS I came to know many young Muslim students on U.S campuses and this led to many invitations to campuses for lectures. Through such lectures, I increased my knowledge of the Muslim communities across the country and soon the nickname "Ibn Battuta" came to be attached to me by some of my colleagues like professor Aziz Batran of Howard University's History Department. The sobriquet was given possibly due to my continuous absence from the University on weekends to give lectures to Muslim students and local communities. Another point that deserves attention here is the fact that within my first four years of membership I was elected to the position of vice president of AMSS. This term of office was eventful and through the cooperation and support of the then president Waheed Fakri, Mumtaz Ahmed and I launched the American Journal of Islamic social sciences (AJISS) in 1984, which is the first Muslim-edited scholarly publication that is not only considered a referred journal, but also a periodical that is indexed by the major social science indexing and abstracting agencies. As we all know, this journal has for some time now been jointly edited and produced by the International Institute of Islamic Thought and AMSS. Its editorial management has changed from Muntaz and I to several of our colleagues who also served as either president or member of the executive board of AMSS. This organ of AMSS has been one of the legitimizing factors of our organization. The younger members must take it to greater heights in the coming years and decades. The third development since my association with AMSS was the discovery of my better half at one of the annual meetings of AMSS. It was indeed at our annual meeting at Purdue University in Lafayette, Indiana, that I met my future wife who was a Fulbright scholar from Thailand then studying community development at the university of Missouri in Columbia, Missouri. This development has changed my life immeasurably and AMSS will always be seen as the body of Muslims that shaped my family life and built a bridge of cultural and spiritual understanding beyond the shores of the North America into the hinterland of Muslim life in Southeast Asia. The fourth development was my election to the post of president. Through such an office, as in the case of the vice-presidency, I learn to cooperate with a wide range of Muslims in the U.S and beyond. In retrospect, I should say that leading AMSS is not an easy task because you are buffeted here and there by the struggle to raise funds and to make sure that panel materialize and members pay their dues and their registration fees at the annual meetings.

Without brothers like Dr. Mushtaqur Rahman and others, neither my presidency nor that of my successors could have amounted to anything. The challenge is still here and we all have to work together to get things done. This is where I will appeal to the younger and new members to accept the challenge and make themselves available for new task and responsibilities. What we call the discipline councils have not materialized the way all of us wanted many years ago, largely because local initiative and active participation of Muslim intellectuals interested in various fields of social science have yet to be properly cultivated.

The fifth development since I joined the ranks of AMSS is my involvement in the creation of new Muslim structures to advance the cause of Islam in the U.S. AMSS has been a rich field for networking for those who understand and speak the language of social interaction among Muslims. Apart from talking to students on various campuses, AMSS network has facilitated our interaction with scholars and community activists around the country. By writing for *Islamic Horizons, Message International* and several other community-based publications I have been able to share the AMSS message with many people who normally do not attend AMSS conferences. This is where and how town and gown meet, and AMSS leaders and members have the responsibility to create such linkages and connections. The sixth development that deserves attention here is the global outreach of AMSS and its impact on me and the others in the organization. As far as I can recall, AMSS has made it a policy to invite Muslim intellectuals and scholars from the Muslim world. Over the years, I have come to know a good number of persons through such engagements. The idea is a good one, and the younger generation of members should do their best to maintain the tradition. It does not only extend the hand of friendship to brothers and sisters overseas, but it also enables us to learn from their researches just as they too gain from our work.

Last but not the least, the seventh development since my association with AMSS has been my greater involvement in interfaith dialogue within the U.S. and around the world. Learning from the examples and experiences of Dr. Ismail Faruqi, the first president of AMSS, some of us have embraced the idea of interfaith and are now actively pushing the frontiers of dialogue between Muslims and other members of the Abrahamic tradition. While doing so, we are mindful of the need to either Islamize knowledge or learn to give an Islamic reading to the growing body of human knowledge. This is the message and vision of AMSS as I have lived and experienced it over the years. Thanks. Was Salaam.

5 THE MISSION AND VISION OF AMSS

Anis Ahmed[5]

The genesis of AMSS can be traced back to the formative phase of the Islamic movement in North America. While Islam was there in the Americas, perhaps before Columbus discovered the new world, a systematic and meaningful institutional approach to disseminate Islam developed in the late sixties. Many Muslim social scientists who were regular participants in national conventions of the Muslim Students Associations from the early sixties felt the need for a professional forum where they could address methodological and strategic issues, within an Islamic framework, in their respective disciplines. Being a part of this process from the very conception of the idea of Islamization of social sciences, perhaps I am privileged to recall our vision of AMSS.

This vision was shared and articulated in our discussions, informal as well as formal, much before the creation of AMSS. Our colleagues among the

---

[5] *Dr. Anis Ahmed is Director of Daw'ah Academy at the International Islamic University Islamabad*

social scientist such as Prof. Ismail al-Faruqi *Shaheed,*
Dr. Eltigani AbuGideiri *marhum*, Dr. AbdulHamid
AbuSulayman, Dr. Syed Zain al-Abidin *marhum,* Dr.
Ilyas Bayunus, Dr. Farid Ahmed, Dr. Monzer Kahf,
Dr. Abdul Haq Ansari, Dr. Mahmoud Rashdan, Dr.
Wasiullah Khan, and Dr. Sayyid M. Syeed, at one
time or another, contributed substantially toward the
development and maturity of the idea.

It is interesting that not only social scientists but
natural and physical scientists like Dr. Ahmad
Totonji, Dr. Jamal Barzinji, and Dr. Hisham al-Talib
offered all possible assistance in building this
community of Muslim intellectuals in North
America. I can vividly recall long hours we spent
together in deliberations on our vision of AMSS.

The beauty of discussion, however, was that we
could all come up with a consensus to discover and
organize Muslim social scientist in North America.
In 1972 with our first formal gathering at the Illinois
Institute of Technology, Chicago, AMSS was
founded. At this gathering for the first time, Muslim
social scientists addressed themselves to the issues of
Islamic methodology for social sciences or
application of Islamic principles in areas such as
economics, psychology, sociology, history and
religion.

For the next six years, as secretary general of AMSS with Prof. Isma'il al-Faruqi as its president, I personally experienced an uphill task of discovering Islam's relevance to social realities and social change, its role in development, and its position on modernity and future of the *ummah*. Every single step in our journey convinced us of the significance of the process of Islamization of knowledge. The discipline groups we formulated helped us in moving in this direction.

Today, when I look back on our formative period, I feel it was the commitment, sincerity, and untiring efforts of the founding fathers, who were inspired by the emphasis of the Islamic movements on Islam as the complete and total way of life, which provided the intellectual foundations for what we are today— after about a quarter of a century of continuous struggle. Many of the colleagues with whom we began this journey have departed particularly, Prof. al-Faruqi and Dr. Eltigani AbuGideiri (*marhum*) who were always in the forefront of our work. Similarly, many of us who were involved since the inception of AMSS are on their way to exit. It is time to make a serious effort to write the history of the idea. At this juncture we also need to consider how AMSS, as a learned society with a mission (*da'wah*) is going to meet the challenge of the 21st century.

The brief message I have for my colleagues, brothers, and sisters in AMSS is to intensify our relation with the intellectual roots of the Association. An association without an ideological foundation is no association. While the association has all liberty to look critically on the strategies, tactics, and even methodology of the Islamic movements, its only justifications to exist is its inseparable intellectual relation with the contemporary Islamic movements.

The emergence of young intellectuals influenced by the works of the founding fathers of the Islamic movements in Pakistan, Egypt, Turkey, Algeria, and elsewhere is a welcome phenomenon. However, this does not marginalize the contribution of these founding fathers like Syed Abdul A'la Maududi, Imam al-Banna al-Shaheed Syed Qutb, Ustaz Malik Bennebi, Prof. Isma'il al-Faruqi and others. While liberating ourselves from hero worship we must remember that the movement for Islamization of knowledge can only be understood in the context of Islamic reawakening kindled by the Islamic movements.

So long as we keep looking critically on their profound contribution we will move forward towards a bright future. An objective evaluation of our first twenty-five years will help us to enter the twenty-first century with a clear vision of our ideology—integration of revealed knowledge, *wahy* with other sciences.

The mission and vision of AMSS call for looking forward in our approach. The real challenge of the twenty-first century is not simply how to preserve and maintain an Islamic character in our social sciences. In a post-socialist and post-modernist world of relativistic values it is our obligation to offer and share with others in the universal axiological paradigm of the Islamic social sciences. The vision of an integrated knowledge, a social science founded on universal Islamic values, is yet to be accomplished.

I have my most sincere and warm prayers for the bright future of AMSS at the threshold of the 21st century.

May Allah guide us always to the right path.

6 MESSAGE FROM THE ISLAMIC SOCIETY OF NORTH AMERICA

Sayyid M. Syeed[6]

We join the 25th celebration of the founding of the Association of Muslim Social Scientists (AMSS) with a sense of pride and gratitude to the Almighty Allah.

AMSS is a gift of the Muslim Students Association (MSA), which evolved into the Islamic Society of North America (ISNA), to the Muslim World and to all humankind. Only in America could such an organization be born. The brain drain from the Muslim world put a large number of Muslim scientists in our midst. It was here that the Muslim intellectuals were challenged with new ideas and paradigms. It became their duty to identify the relevance of Islam to their academic disciplines and work for a reconstruction of Islamic thought individually and collectively.

The new direction in Islamic thought that AMSS initiated has spread from country to country and *from South M. Syeed is Secretary General of the Islamic Society of North America*

Islamize various disciplines and to reestablish an authentic tradition based on revelation, Islamic heritage, and contemporary developments are going to provide the validity and a sense of direction that we need for new millennium.

The close cooperation between ISNA and its progeny AMSS will ensure an involvement of a larger number of social scientists in the great task that AMSS has, It will also provide outreach to the largest segments of Muslims in America to absorb the insights understanding of Islam free from stereotypes and stagnation.

APPENDIX

CONFERENCE PROGRAM
IN THE SILVER JUBILEE YEAR

The Twenty-Fifth Annual Conference

The Association of Muslim Social Scientists

Herndon, Virginia

October 26-27, 1996

FRIDAY, OCTOBER 26, 1996

6:00 – 8:00 p.m.

TRANSPORTING AMSS SPEAKERS TO SISS
& PRAYER
& SISS INAUGURAL

SESSION I
8:15 – 8:30 p.m.

OPENING SESSION

SISS Library - Chair: Mushtaqur Rahman

Mushtaqur Rahman, AMSS President
Taha Jabir Al-Alwani, SISS President
Iqbal Unus, Conference Chairman

SESSION II
8:15 – 10:00 p.m.

Panel 1: Educational/Learning Models
SISS Library – Chair: M. A. W. Fakhri

Zayid Abdul-Karim – *"Understanding the Islamic Conversion Experiences of Two African American Males: A Case Study Approach to Decision making For Transformational Change"*

Hakim M. Rashid – *"The Educator's Islamic Demeanor Scale (EIDS): An Islamic Framework for Evaluating the Behavior of Muslim Educators"*

SATURDAY, OCTOBER 26, 1996

SESSION III
9:00-10:30 a.m.

Panel 2: Islam and the West: The Media & Academia
Room A   Chair: Anas Al-Shaikh Ali

Ralph Coury - *"Neo-Modernization Theory and its Search for Enemies: The Role of the Arab And Islam"*

Dilnawaz Siddiqui – *"Theories of Agenda-setting: Do or*

Should Muslims Have Any?

Behrooz Kalantari – *"Media and the Paradox of Bureaucratic Politics"*

Sharaf Rahman – *"Media Education and the Muslim World"*

Panel 3: Islamic Resurgence: From Indonesia to Egypt

Room B   Chair: Iiyas Bayunus

Hazem Ghobarah – *"Within Country Comparisons: A Quantitative Intra-Country Comparison of the Islamic Movement in Egypt"*

Ismail Hakki Goksoy – *"The Policy of the Dutch Government Towards Islam in Indonesia"*

Ghulam M. Haniff – *"The Future of Islam in the Former Yugoslavia"*

SESSION IV
10:45 a.m. – 12:15 p.m.

Panel 4: The Role of Islam in Development

Room A   Chair: Ghulam Haniff

Mazen Hashem – *"Levels of Knowledge and Interculteration: Implications for development and for the*

Islamization of Knowledge"

Ashraful Hasan – *"Islam and Social Change: A comparative Analysis of Malaysia and Bangladash"*

Panel 5: Islamic Economics
Room B   Chair: Suleyman Akdemir

Suleyman Akdemir - *"A New Approach for Protecting Victims Based On Social Solidarity: The System Of Akile*

M. Kabir Hassan – *"A Nonparametric Cost Structure Analysis of Traditional Commercial and Islamic Banks in Bangladash"*

Arif Ersoy – "Islam and the New International Order"

Aslam M. Haneef – *"The Concept and Practical Dimension of Islamization of Knowledge – A Case Study of the Economic programme, IIUM"*

SESSION V 12:30-2.00 p.m.

PRAYER/LUNCH
&
AL-FARUQI MEMORIAL LECTURE

ADAMS Center   Chair: Salahuddin Malik

Speaker: John Voll
Center for Muslim-Christian Understanding
Georgetown University

SESSION VI
2:15-3:30 p.m.

Panel 6: Islamization of Knowledge
Room A Chair: Dilnawaz Siddiqui

Hira Karagulle – *"Analogous Analysis of Natural, Social and Religious Sciences"*

Mustapha Achoui – *"Social Sciences and Religion: What is Relationship?"*

Panel 7: Islam and the psychological & Evolution of Man
Room B Chair: Wasiullah Khan

Nizar al-Ani – *"A basic Plan to Islamicize Psychology"*

M. Akhtar – *"Psychotherapeutic Significance in Beliefs and Practices of Islam"*

Ismail Yakit – *"The creation of Man and His Evolution in the Qur'an"*

SESSION VII
3:45 – 5:15 p.m.

Panel 8: Shari'ah

Room A   Chair: Taha Jabir Alalwani

Abdul Basit – *"Shariah and Contemporary Issues"*

Shweish Mahameed – *"The Justice of the Witness: Two perspectives on Islamic Shariah and Sociology"*

Panel 9: TBA
Room B

SESSION VIII
5:30 – 6:30 p.m.

Anniversary and Business Session
26 Years of AMSS

Mushtaqur Rahman, President

SESSION IX
6:30 -7:00 p.m.

PRAYER & BREAK

```
┌─────────────────────────────────────────┐
│            SESSION X                      │
│          7:00 – 9:00 p.m.                 │
│                                           │
└─────────────────────────────────────────┘
```

AMSS BANQUET

ADAMS Center   Chair: Mushtaqur Rahman

Keynote Speaker: Clovis Maksoud
Center for the study of the Global South
American University

SUNDAY, OCTOBER 27, 1996

```
┌─────────────────────────────────────────┐
│            SESSION XI                     │
│          9:00 – 10:30 a.m.                │
│                                           │
└─────────────────────────────────────────┘
```

Panel 10: Islam and the West: Political & Aesthetic
Discourse

Room A   Chair: Mumtaz Ahmad

Mohammed A. Muqtedar Khan & Naisy Sarduy –
*"Islam and the West: The Discourse and the Politics of the
Threat"*

Omar Nasim – *"A Contrast Between Western Aesthetic
Theory and Islamic Aesthetics: Kantian Dualism and the
Islamic Unicity Principle"*

SESSION XII
10:30 – 11:30 a.m.

CONCLUDING REMARKS

AMSS EXECUTIVE MEETING

Room A   Chair: Mushtaqur Rahman

Intellectual Engagement

ABOUT THE COMPILER/EDITOR

Dr. Iqbal Unus [Ph.D, Emory University 1977] has focused his professional career on the evolving Muslim presence in America, gaining distinctive insight into its growth. He is associated with the International Institute of Islamic Thought, and has served as secretary general of the Islamic Society of North America, where he is currently member of the Board. He has been conferred community service awards by the Islamic Society of North America (ISNA) and the Council of American-Islamic Relations (CAIR). He is also a fellow at the Alwaleed Center for Muslim-Christian Understanding (ACMCU) at Georgetown University and director-at-large at the United Nations Association of the National Capital Area (UNA-NCA